Remembrances

A Written and Illustrated Coloring Book for Adults

LEAH PALM

Illustrator: James Schoppe

To order additional copies of this book, contact:
Xlibris
1-888-795-4274
www.Xlibris.com
Orders@Xlibris.com

ISBN: Softcover   978-1-6641-1948-2
        EBook   978-1-6641-1921-5

Print information available on the last page

Rev. date: 07/29/2020

Remembrances

A Written and Illustrated Coloring Book for Adults

LEAH PALM

Illustrator: James Schoppe

ACKNOWLEDGEMENT

The author would like to acknowledge her friends who shared their personal like experiences so others could enjoy and smile at their true stories.

These people include Debra Ueker, Ollie Burnet, Winona Williams, Helen O'Galagher, Christine Palm, Mary Jane Weiss, Rosie Cano, and Leah Palm. Some contributors had more than one story to tell, even though everyone initially said they had no stories.

I also must thank Fareeda Gibbons for her typing of multiple drafts and the final copy. She did a wonderful job of editing everything I wrote.

Lastly, I thank my publisher Xlibris, 1-888-795-2474, for encouraging me to see this book through to its finalization.

Leah Palm

DEDICATION

This book is dedicated to my mother, Christine J. Palm, who had a wonderful sense of humor.

I would also like to dedicate this book to James and Victoria Schoppe. Without whom there would be no illustrations to bring the stories to life.

And I would like to dedicate this book to Linsa G. Funderburg, M.D. for giving me the Dr. Seuss book, "Oh the Places You'll Go". It motivated me to complete this project.

In addition, I dedicate this book to my reader who I hope will enjoy it as much as I did while writing it.

INTRODUCTION

Welcome to *Remembrances*. All stories are nonfictional with a few necessary fictional name changes and fictional embellishments.

This coloring book is created for the pleasure of adults. Please enjoy the stories and their illustrations. May they stimulate your remembrances of earlier years.

Pictures and stories are perforated so you may remove and frame them.

CONTENTS

Wilbur The Box Turtle (Tortoise)

The Willoughbys, a family of five, included Mom and Dad and three sisters. They used to take a leisurely ride through the country every Sunday. One Sunday, they saw a box turtle laboriously crossing the road. So they topped the car, picked up the turtle, and took the turtle home. He was placed in the backyard.

The first thing they did is name him Wilbur. They placed food and water out for him. He located the nourishment and made himself at home. Every winter he would hibernate and show up the next spring.

One winter, he lost his way and had mistakenly dug under the fence. So the five family members organized a search committee for him. They went from house to house and finally found him.

One day a daughter picked Wilbur up and watched him pull his feet and head in and completely close his shell. Thinking she had scared him, she placed him back on the grass. The next day she picked him up again. However, instead of setting him down, she gently rubbed his underside. Much to her surprise, he slowly pushed his feet out and stuck his head out. Then Wilbur allowed her to caress him on his head. From that day forward, Wilbur never left the yard as far as they knew. However, daily, when the screen door opened, he would stretch his head above the grass and slowly move toward the door to eat and get his belly rubbed.

The Race

It was a usual school day in Georgia in the year 1944. I was in the first grade. My dad was in the army, and my mom was a housewife who did a lot of canning.

I was skipping home from school when I spied our neighbor's goat that was tied to a post in his front yard.

One of my greatest pleasures on the way home from school was to tease this goat. So I would edge up to him and run back. I did this several times. Much to my surprise, his rope broke, and he came after me. He was holding his head down and charging.

I ran as fast as my short legs could carry me. I started yelling for my dad. I saw him open the front screen door, and I ran between his legs. The goat followed me, but Dad caught him by his horns and pushed him back. I was saved. I never told Dad why the goat chased me.

First Chair

Roger had a desire to play an alto sax around the year 1949. At that time, a new saxophone cost $185, much more than his parents could afford. However, overtime, the family scraped together the amount. They purchased him a Morton Alto Saxophone, which he still has. However, it is no longer playable.

Roger was a mature teenager and appreciated his parents' sacrifice. As a result, Roger practiced daily and concentrated on his technique and rhythm. The results of his commitment to practicing found him as first chair saxophone in his freshman, sophomore, and senior years of high school. Being first chair gave him the pleasure and responsibility of playing the required solos. Additionally, Roger enjoyed playing in the marching and concert bands. He even played in the all district and all regional bands.

Roger attended Texas A&I, now Texas A&M, in Kingsville, Texas, and graduated. In his first year, he played in the college marching band. He also was a member of a dance band called The Blue Notes. His talent earned him a three-year music tuition scholarship, even though he was a nonmusic major. Now he is retired and only plays for his friends and himself. What a wonderful talent to take into his retirement years.

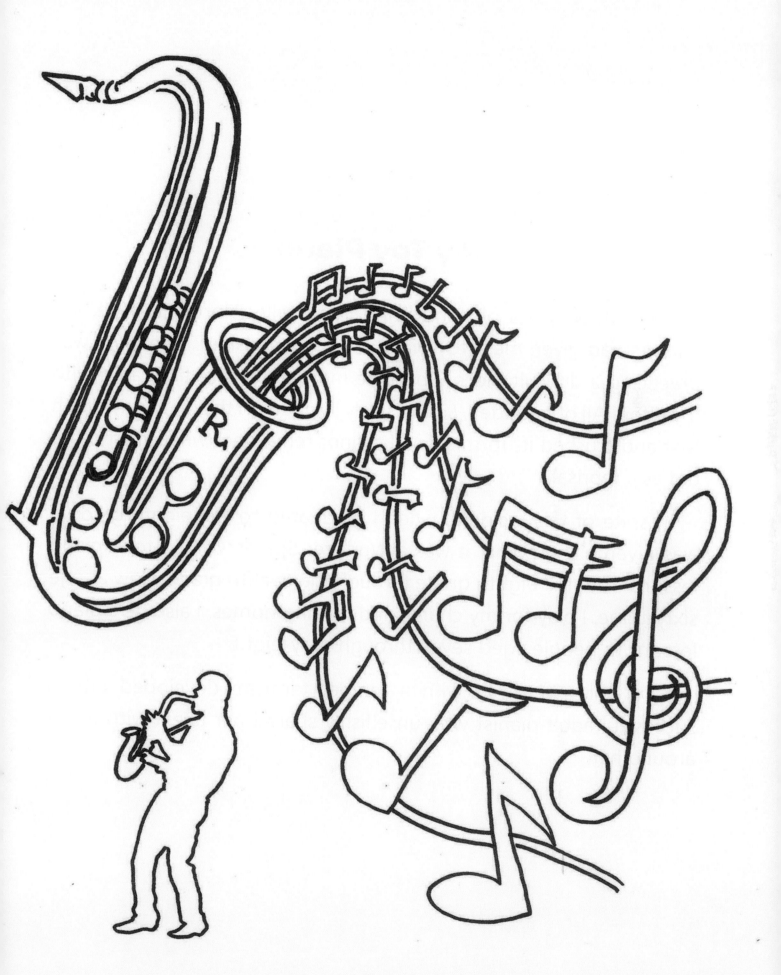

My Toy Piano

I was three years old and living in Ashville, North Carolina. My parents had given me a toy piano, which I cherished. One day I was practicing a difficult piece. I became more and more frustrated with my effort. All of a sudden, I impulsively jumped on the piano with both feet and crushed it. To this day, I cannot remember what my mother did as a reprisal.

In spite of this incident, when I graduated to the eighth grade, I was given a real piano. It was a Wurlitzer Spinet. On it, I took piano lessons from the eighth grade through the twelfth grade. Now at age sixty-three, I play for my church and nursing homes. I also give piano lessons to people aged seven through sixty-eight.

So a three-year-old with a temper tantrum developed into a successful adult pianist who unselfishly shared her talent with those around her.

You're in the Army Now

In the 1970s, I found myself in the army at Camp Bullis, Fort Sam Houston, San Antonio, Texas. We were having field exercises. It was humid, hot, dusty, and with no breeze.

After attending several lectures, learning to read maps, and performing several military maneuvers, it was time to return to our usual work routine. We were told the bus would pick us up at Point A. I arose at 0400 hours, showered, and dressed. I arose this early because I did not want everyone to see me dragging my duffel bag to Point A instead of carrying it to Point A.

I was struggling with my duffel bag when a helpful sergeant asked me if he could carry my duffel bag for me. I, being an officer and a leader, had to say, "No, thank you."

So sweating and about to collapse, I started dragging my duffel bag. Then an experienced sergeant walked up behind me, grabbed my duffel bag, and said, "Come on, Captain." I stepped smartly in behind him and followed him to Point B. All I could think was Thank goodness for seasoned sergeants. What would the army do without them? What would I do without them?

Unbelievable

Late in the 1970s, my friend and I took off from Fort Leonard Wood, Missouri, toward Junction City, Kansas. We decided to drive my silver Volkswagen Beetle. I treasured this little car. It had black leather seats and a sunroof. I loved driving it in the snow and on long trips.

This trip to Kansas was to spend Christmas with my parents. We were at my parents when one evening a huge thunderstorm developed. Lightning was streaking across the sky, and thunder was clapping like two cymbals. All of a sudden, we heard a loud cracking and then a thud.

I had moved my Beetle to the backyard for safekeeping. Upon rushing to the backyard, we saw a large tree limb lying on top of the Beetle. My heart sank. But much to my surprise, after removing the limb, there were neither dents nor scratches. I was relieved and treasured my dome-shaped Beetle even more.

Nature's Show

One spring day in San Antonio, Texas, a barn swallow dive-bombed me as I exited my front door. She had been busy building a nest under the front door cover. She was using mud pellets, feathers, and grass to construct her concave, cup-shaped nest. It was a beautiful striated nest. No engineer could have constructed it better. In time, she laid her reddish spotted white eggs.

Soon, in about eighteen to twenty-three days, a brood of five barn swallows was born. I watched them stretch their necks up and open their triangular yellow beaks to be fed. The mother would drop insects and flies in their mouths. Time passed and I noticed that after they ate, they would turn around, place their backsides over the rim of the nest, and defecate. I thought, What clean little birds and what a mess they make!

Next, they had to learn to fly. They jumped from the nest to my night light, defecated on it, and flew on their way. Every spring they would replicate the nature show at least twice.

Pekin Ducks

(Domestic Ducks)

In 1873, the Pekin duck was imported from China to the United States of America by James Palmer of Stonington, Connecticut.

During the mid-eighties, some Pekin ducks were seen swimming in a narrow river behind some residences in Libertyville, Illinois. One day they strolled up on a lady's patio. They waited there. Nothing happened, so they waddled back to the river. Unbeknownst to them, an eighty-nine-year-old lady was observing them. So when they returned the next day, she was ready to feed them.

Out she went down the hill to the river with the ducks following. She threw the corn in the river. One by one, the ducks slipped into the water, ate the corn, and swam away. The ducks repeated this scenario for three weeks until they swam away for the last time.

"The Parrot Goes!"

My father who was a sergeant in the army and my mom and I lived on Fort Gulick in the Panama Canal Zone. This was during the Korean War in the 1950s. My father was in charge of the structural fi res. At his fi re station, he housed an aggressive parrot. One day he decided to bring the parrot home.

As we were eating dinner one evening, the parrot named Sarge flew from my dad's shoulder to mine. I was afraid of the parrot and asked to have it removed. Before it was taken off my shoulder, it bit my left ear. I left the table crying.

Being only thirteen, I had no say-so about the parrot. So he continued to stay with us until the day he chased my mom up the stairwell. The parrot was screaming and flogging her with his wings. Dad had to wrestle the parrot off Mom. She collected herself, turned toward Dad and said, "The parrot goes!"

Daisy

In the 1970s, there was a cat named Daisy. She was a tortoise shell cat who lived on Bloomdale Street in San Antonio, Texas. She was usually busy educating one of her two annual litters. However, this day found her sunning and relaxing.

She suddenly stood in a stiff upright position like a cat will do. Every so often, she would quickly turn her head and reach down behind her. Then she would jerk her head back up. She did this repeatedly for several minutes. It turned out she was grabbing a green grass snake, pulling it partway out of its hole, then letting it go. Finally, she tired of the game and quit.

After playing with the snake, Daisy remembered her responsibility to school her kittens. Daisy began her vocalizations to gather the kittens together. The kittens opened their eyes and lazily placed themselves in a semicircle in front of Daisy. Daisy increased her vocalizations, demonstrated washing her face, and observed the kittens doing the same. However, a yellow and white kitten named Fritz wasn't paying attention. As a result, Daisy reached over and whacked him in the head. Fritz delightfully joined the group and began washing his face.

Daisy

One Tough Grandmother

In Donahue, Iowa, around 2010, a sixty-seven-year-old grandmother named Holly was pulling out of a farm road onto a highway. As she entered the highway, a large garbage truck was traveling down the highway and crashed into Holly's Ford Escape. The passenger side door was driven across to the driver's side and compressed Holly. Luckily, the lady truck driver was not injured, so she immediately called 911. Soon, Holly was driven to the hospital where the physician disclosed that Holly had multiple fractures to include brain trauma. As a result, Holly was hospitalized and was put on rehab for several months.

During this time, her granddaughter, Debbie, visited her faithfully. During these trips, Debbie tried to energize Holly, but nothing seemed to work until Debbie brought a coloring book and crayons to the hospital.

This gesture reminded Holly of the times she and Debbie used to color together when Debbie was about six years old. The coloring activity seemed to stimulate Holly, and she brightened up. Soon, she was discharged home. After a recuperative period, Holly resumed working at a friend's farm, where she took care of the goats and chickens.

Even though Holly had lost some memory and suffered with residual pain, she never complained because she was one tough grandmother.

My Blue and White Schwinn Bicycle

Circa 1950, I spent much of my free time riding a blue and white Schwinn bicycle.

I would come home from school, sit in my red rocker, do my homework, and eat homemade chocolate chip cookies. Then I would change from my school clothes to my play clothes.

Later, I would ride to the top of the steep hill in front of our house. I would peddle rapidly down the hill. When my tires were rolling fast enough to balance the bike, I would cautiously release my grasp on the handle bars, place my feet, one at a time, on the bike seat. Then I would stand upright on the seat.

As I flew down the hill, I would listen for the train whistle. At a specified landmark, I would slowly raise my arms away from my sides. Then down the hill I would fly, racing the train to the track crossing. Miraculously, I did this successfully many times. What luck!

The Long Green Eel

During the 1950s, my dad would drive over a threatening narrow bridge that permitted us to cross from the Atlantic side to the Pacific side of the Panama Canal.

After crossing over, we arrived at the coral reef where we wished to fi sh. Dad went to the edge of the deep water to catch barracuda and large red snappers. I, wearing my dad's combat boots, went to the shallow side. Immediately, I saw a green eel projecting his head in and out of a rough-edged coral hole. I wondered if he could be caught. I baited my hook with shrimp and dangled it in front of the eel's head. Initially, he wasn't interested. I slowly moved the shrimp away from him as he tentatively edged out a little further each time. Then suddenly the eel lunged out of the coral reef and grabbed the bait.

Frightened and not knowing what to do with the rapidly gyrating and contorting catch at the end of my rod, I yelled for my dad. He came running across the reef, cut the eel free, and saved me. I caught no more eels.

Mia's First Oyster

On or about 1943, somewhere in Georgia, the Quickliters were sitting on their weathered front porch. Mrs. Quickliter was wearing her unraveled straw hat and smoking her corncob pipe as she rocked in her chair. Mr. Quickliter was sitting in his rocker and smoking his corncob pipe too. It was a lazy sunny afternoon.

The Quickliters had rented out half of their duplex to military family who had a six-year-old girl named Mia. It being a quiet day, the Quickliters decided to go to the backyard and shuck some oysters. Mia watched them and repeatedly pestered Mr. Quickliter to give her one. So he did. He also told her if he put an oyster in her mouth, she could not spit it out. Mia agreed.

In went the oyster. Mia's cheeks puffed out. She turned red in the face. Just in time, her mother called and told her to spit out the oyster. Mia never pestered Mr. Quickliter again.

The Bantam Hen

When I was in the fifth grade, my parents gave me an allowance to do outside chores. One of the jobs was to care for and feed our chickens. So daily, I would clean the fenced-in pen and collect eggs from the nests sitting on the wooden perches. I also fed and watered the chickens. Once a month, I would whitewash the chicken coop.

Among the chickens was my pet Bantam hen. One day I noticed food falling out of her craw. I yelled for Dad. He came running and evaluated the situation. Next thing I knew, my dad had Banty in one hand and a needle and thread in the other. He sewed Banty's craw closed, and she ate fi ne the next day and every day thereafter.

A Father's Love

During WWII, Mary was seven years old and wanted a bicycle. At that time, because of the war effort, a bicycle was a difficult commodity to come by.

However, her parents found one that a neighbor possessed and no longer rode. So they purchased it for Mary. Now Mary had to learn to ride it. This was no easy challenge for her, especially since the only roads she had to practice riding on were seashell roads along the Texas coast.

Well, her father, being a teacher, was not one to give up easily. He located a forty- to fifty-foot length of concrete. He then spent many days holding on to the bicycle seat, walking Mary back and forth until she finally was able to ride alone. Such is a father's love.

Paper Dolls

Carmen was a seven-year-old second grader. It was 1954, and Carmen lived in San Antonio, Texas. She passed time by playing with her paper dolls. Almost every day she would spread her beloved dolls over her bed and, one by one, change their outfits.

Another activity Carmen enjoyed was going shopping downtown with her elder sister. Carmen would help her sister by carrying packages. The elder sister thanked Carmen by purchasing her a new set of paper dolls. The new set was usually purchased at Kress and Co. or Woolworths.

These trips occurred over a three-year period. Carmen collected over one hundred paper dolls. The collection included Shirley Temple and Blondie and Dagwood dolls. When Carmen wanted to increase her collection, she cut out paper dolls from the McCall's magazine.

Then one day, at ten years old, she became embarrassed because she was told she was too old to play with paper dolls. So she put them away. But Carmen never lost her love for paper dolls. Now as an adult, this love has manifested itself into a collection of valuable real dolls, whose eyes open and close.

Kite Flying as a Respite

During the mid-eighties, Shelly and Kathleen Omar went to the Galveston, Texas coast. They wanted to observe the sport and/or the stunt kite-flying competition. They observed single kites and multilined sport kites that could be maneuvered from various directions.

The Omars were approximately in their forties. They were enthralled with the breathtaking kite maneuvers. The kites climbed and dipped and dived. As a result, they bought their first sport kite. Shelly flew it a lot. As a matter of fact, he liked it so well that he bought his second sport kite at the Port Aransas, Texas Kite Festival. His interest in kite flying lasted quite a while. However, soon his busy schedule forced him to store his kites.

Then surprisingly, the business for which he worked went bankrupt. This shutdown forced Shelly to temporarily live apart from his wife. So he found a job in a large city, and he purchased a condominium. He lived there Monday through Friday and traveled home on the weekends.

To fulfill his free time, Monday through Friday, Shelly returned to kite flying. It helped the time pass. And he knew this would be his respite.

The Whelping Room

In the mid-1950s, in Junction City, Kansas, Josie decided to mate her two German shepherds named Jana and Duke. Hence, she set up a whelping room that was warm, safe, and comfortable for Jana.

The two shepherds mated, and sixty-three days later, ten puppies were born. When Jana whelped her ninth and tenth pup, she was exhausted and unable to break the birth sacks. So Josie split the sacks for her, wiped the pups clean, and placed them on her nipples. All the pups appeared healthy.

The third pup had turned out to be a pure white German shepherd. This was a rare sight. Josie allowed all the pups to exercise in the large kitchen.

Finally, the day came for Josie to sell the pups. So she advertised her pups for sale. Slowly, each pup was sold to a loving home. This litter was the end of the whelping room.

Doc the Veterinarian

I had just finished six years of sacrifice and hard study and signed my life away to build a new veterinary clinic. I had mixed feelings and was proud of what I had accomplished but somewhat anxious about how this was going to work out.

My very first client was an upset lady who appeared in my office carrying an injured puppy. Along with her were two small boys, maybe seven or eight, both crying. The puppy had been struck by a car, and it was obvious to me that it had a broken leg. We proceeded to the exam room, and she directed the boys to remain in the reception area. I examined the puppy and explained to her the procedure for repair, treatment, and cost. She stated these boys' father died two weeks ago, and there was no way she could afford the treatment. She said also, "I already told the boys we would have to put the puppy down."

Being a new vet, I wasn't prepared for a situation like this. But I knew there was no way I was going to destroy that puppy. All my life, I had been taught to do the right thing, so I told the young mother to leave the puppy and not to worry about the expense. The case turned out great, and everyone was relieved and happy.

About fifteen years later, a young man walked into my office and introduced himself. He said, "You don't know me, but I never forgot what you did for me and my brother, and I want to pay you for taking care of our puppy." When my wife passed away, one of the first people to call me was that same kind young man. You can never go wrong doing the right thing.

THE END

Printed in the United States
By Bookmasters